ART AND HISTORY OF
NAZARETH
CANA-MOUNT TABOR-MEGIDDO

Text by
EUGENIO ALLIATA
Studium Biblicum Franciscanum

D1297886

BONECHI & STEIMATZKY

Translated by Julia Weiss

The cover of this book, designed by the Casa Editrice Bonechi graphic artists, is protected by international copyright.

Photographs from the archives of Casa Editrice Bonechi taken by Paolo Giambone.
The photo on page 2 is a courtesy of Albatross Aerial Photography, Tel Aviv.

ISBN 88-8029-309-5

* * *

INTRODUCTION

A flourishing city in the lower Galilee, the mountains that crown northern Israel; a young Jewish maiden betrothed to an artisan descended from the House of David; a divine messenger announces that mankind's long expectation will be fulfilled; thirty years of silence, and hiding for Christ before he would begin preaching the advent of the Kingdom of God among men; goal of pilgrims from the world over for centuries. All of this is Nazareth. Ancient human remains discovered in the cave of el-Qafze, a rocky ridge southeast of the city prove that the Nazareth area has been inhabited since prehistoric times (Paleolithic era: 500,000-100,000 B.C.). Tombs with bronze tools and pottery dating from the early part of the second millenium B.C. were discovered near the site of the Church of the Annunciation. Other household items from the days of the kings of Israel (IX-VIII cent. B.C.), further evidence that the area was inhabited during Old Testament times, were found in several places. From Jesus' era there are tombs and houses, even though the continuity of life in the area has clouded the traces of the Gospel Nazareth more than a little. The city did not play any significant role in the Jewish revolt against Rome described by the Jewish historian Josephus Flavius (66-70 A.D.) even though the first part of the war took place nearby. The Ha-Pizzez, a Jewish family of priestly descent—those who served in the Temple of Jerusalem—are recorded as having lived in the city when imperial Roman power was reestablished (II-III cent. A.D.). We must admit, however, that Nazareth would not have had any more than a very minor role in history if it had not been the home of Jesus the Nazarene. In the local languages Christians in general are called Nazarenes (Nazâra in Arabic and Nozerim in Hebrew). According to one historically plausible hypothesis, Jewish followers of Christ (from the sect of the Nazarenes or Ebionites) and Jesus' own relatives maintained an ancient place of Christian worship known to the early pilgrims as "Mary's House". Then came the Byzantine churches (V century) and the crusaders (XII cent.) who maintained religious traditions in the town. The crusaders' church, decorated with fine sculptures was reduced to rubble by the Mamaluke sultan Baybars in 1263. After this period it became increasingly difficult for Christians to visit the city and they were forced to pay taxes and duties. In 1620 the Druse emir of Sidon, Fakhr ed-Din, who was quite benevolent towards Christians, allowed the Franciscan order to take care of the sanctuary. But only in 1730 did the Moslem authorities give permission to build a small church over the Grotto of the Annunciation which, though somewhat modified, is still used today. In 1953 the Franciscan Custody of the Holy Land was able to launch construction of the new Sanctuary of the Incarnation. This provided an excellent opportunity for organized archeological research (1955-1966) under the direction of a renowned archeologist, Father Bellarmino Bagatti. The results of these excavations shed new light on the religious and civic history of the land of Jesus. The new basilica, designed by the Italian architect Giovanni Muzio was made possible thanks to contributions from all Catholics and the cooperation of countless artists from all over the world. Structurally "grafted" onto the walls of the crusader basilica, the new building was conceived as a treasure chest to hold and show the world evidence of centuries of reverent love for Mary, Jesus' Mother. May each pilgrim who comes to this harbor of peace, bear the same feelings and love in his heart. Cana, Mount Tabor and the biblical city of Megiddo, three places near Nazareth, overlooking the great Plain of Esdraelon, form the geographic and biblical culmination of this book.

NAZARETH

At the foot of the hill on which the Jewish settlement (Nazèret 'Illit, pop. 38,000) is located and in the midst of the Arab quarter (an-Nâsira, pop. 61,000 part Christian and part Moslem) stands the impressive new Basilica of the Annunciation.

THE CHURCH OF THE ANNUNCIATION

No matter from which direction visitors enter the lovely valley where Nazareth lays, their eyes are immediately drawn to a single monument which is outstanding for its size and unusual architecture. The Church of the Annunciation towers not only over the maze of private homes around it, but also over the large Franciscan monastery that stretches alongside of it. The massive, square base brings to mind the walls of a fortress, but the elegant octagonal drum, topped by the truncated-conical cupola with open lantern lead to thoughts and aspirations of the supernatural world. As Eutychius of Alexandria (IX cent.) wrote in the first part of his *Kitâb al-burhân* or *The Book of Proof*:

"Christ also bequeathed us his relics and the places that witnessed his holiness on earth, and as a pledge of the kingdom of heaven and the delights of the future life that he promised us...In this way, the church of Nazareth which is in the Galilee in the region of the Jordan River, bears witness to the annunciation to Mary by the Archangel Gabriel that she would

conceive the Christ".

The basilica as it stands today was built for the Custody of the Holy Land by the Israeli firm, Solel Boneh of Tel Aviv to plans by the Italian architect, Professor Giovanni Muzio of Milan. The work itself was done by the skilled Christian and Moslem masons and carvers of Nazareth under the direction of the Franciscan architect, Father Benedetto Antonucci. Actual construction was begun on 30 September 1960 when the contract was signed, and the basilica was consecrated by Gabriel Cardinal Garrone on 23 March 1969. Sixty-five meters long, twenty-seven wide and fifty-five high, it is the biggest building of its kind in the Middle East. On his pilgrimage to the Holy Land, Pope Paul VI visited the work site and celebrated Mass in the Holy Grotto on 5 January 1964. In memory of the pope's visit, the city of Nazareth renamed its main street that runs along the base of the hill where the complex stands, for Paul VI.

The main façade was decorated by the Italian sculp-

The western façade of the basilica is dedicated to the mystery of the Incarnation "And the Word was made flesh, and dwelt among us" (John, 1:14). The Annunciation to Mary is the first act in the miraculous story of salvation.

tor Angelo Biancini of Faenza. At the top, the 3 meter tall bronze statue of Christ giving his blessing, is the protagonist of the mystery of the Incarnation celebrated by this façade. "But when the fulness of the time was come, God sent forth his son, born of a woman, made under the law To redeem them that were under the law that we might receive the adoption of the sons" (*Galatians*, 4:4-5). Below, carved into the stones of the façade, the Annunciation, with the words of the Gospel in Latin "Angelus domini nuntiavit Mariae" "The angel of God spoke unto Mary", and in the center, the four evangelists with their symbols, the angel, the lion, the ox and the eagle. On either side, Latin inscriptions of the Old Testament prophecies: "And the Lord God said unto the serpent...it shall bruise thy head and thou shalt bruise his heel" (*Genesis* 3:15) and "Behold, a virgin shall conceive and bear a son, and shall call his name Immanuel" (*Isaiah*, 7:14). The four pink stone bands that run along the façade

with the inscriptions contain representations of the four elements. According to the ancient cosmography they comprised the bands or heavens that Christ would have to cross in order to reach us: fire, air, water and earth. There are also other ancient Christian symbols such as the "cosmic cross" in a circle, or with crosses or flowers or mere points in the four sections created by the arms of the cross. It is the symbol of universal Redemption, manifested through the redeeming strength of the cross that reaches to the four regions of the world. The current "Holy Land Cross" (with five crosses) is merely one of the variations of the cosmic cross. The Greek letters X (*chi*) and P (*rho*), the first two letters of Christ's name, entwined, are carved into the porphyry architrave.
The second protagonist of the mystery commemorated at Nazareth is Mary, to whom the angel spoke and who was asked to be the Savior's mother. The smaller, southern façade is dedicated to her. In the

6

The western façade is decorated with many artworks. The hammered copper and bronze center door was done by the German sculptor, Roland Friedrichsen of Munich.

The scenes depict the life of Christ (from top to bottom on the left, from bottom to top on the right): The Nativity, the Flight into Egypt (detail), working as a carpenter in Nazareth, Baptism by John (detail) preaching (detail), death on the cross.

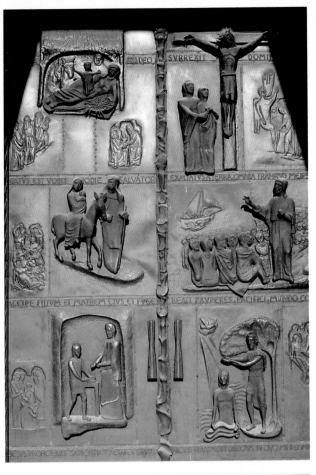

The smaller, southern façade is dedicated to Mary, with the Latin words of the Salve Regina carved into the wall. The portico that goes around the western and southern sides of the building contains many paintings of sanctuaries dedicated to the Virgin in countries around the world.

central niche stands a bronze statue (by the Italian sculptor Franco Verroca of Rome) portraying Mary as the young woman she actually was at the time of the events recounted in the Gospel.

The words of the *Salve Regina*, the ancient prayer that thousands of pilgrims love to recite here, fill the entire façade with their poetry: *Salve, Regina, Mater misericordiae, vita, dulcedo, et spes nostra, salve. Ad te clamamus exsules filii Hevae. Ad te suspiramus gementes et flentes in hac lacrymarum valle. Eia ergo, advocata nostra, illos tuos misericordes oculos ad nos converte. Et Jesum benedictum fructum ventris tui, nobis, post hoc exilium ostende. O clemens, O pia, O dulcis Virgo Maria.*

(Hail, holy queen, Mother of Mercy; hail, our life, our sweetness, and our hope! To thee do we cry, poor banished children of Eve; to thee do we send up our sighs, mourning and weeping in this vale of tears. Turn then, most gracious advocate, thine eyes of mercy towards us; and after this, our exile, show unto us the blessed fruit of thy womb, Jesus. O clement, O loving, O sweet Virgin Mary.)

In front of the Holy Grotto one can almost feel the mystery that took place here so long ago; archeological remains carry us back to a story that dates from the early days of Christianity.

THE GROTTO OF THE ANNUNCIATION

The lower basilica encloses, and provides access insofar as possible, to the site of the Annunciation and archeological finds that bear witness to the long history of Christian worship. Something from each of the buildings that preceded the current structure has been kept visible. From the Franciscan church of 1730 there is the altar of the Holy Grotto; from the crusader church (XII cent.) there are the smaller granite columns that mark off the "Angel's Chapel", and the other larger columns that support the pillars of the nave, and the northern wall of the church which is the back of the grotto. The column bases which now support the main altar and some of the mosaics probably date from the Byzantine church (V cent.) of which the apse is still visible on the eastern side. The wall facing the grotto, the mosaics of "the crown" and "of Conon" as well as the floral paintings and ancient inscriptions in the little grotto along the southern wall of the Grotto of the Annunciation date from the pre-Byzantine structure (III-IV cent.). Other remains of this, the oldest, building can be seen in the museum. One of the most outstanding is the column base with the graffito inscription "Ch[air]e(=Hail) Mary", in the fragment of the column inscribed "at the sanctuary of M[ary]".

The Grotto of the Annunciation, now a chapel, is all that remains of the house where the angel appeared before Mary. The XVIII century altar bears the Latin inscription "Verbum caro hic factum est-This is where the Word became flesh".

In the sixth month the angel Gabriel was sent from God unto a city of Galilee, named Nazareth, to a virgin espoused to man whose name was Joseph of the house of David and the virgin's name was Mary. And the angel came in unto her, and said "Hail, thou that art highly favored, the Lord is with thee". And when she saw him, she was troubled at his saying and cast in her mind what manner of salutation this should be. And the angel said unto her, Fear not Mary: for thou hast found favor with God. And, behold, thou shalt conceive in thy womb, and bring forth a son, and shalt call his name Jesus. He shall be great, and shall be called the Son of the Highest: and the Lord God shall give unto him the throne of his father David: And he shall reign over the house of Jacob forever; and of his kingdom there shall be no end. Then Mary said unto the angel, How shall this be, seeing I know not a man? And the angel answered The Holy Ghost shall come upon thee and the power of the Highest shall overshadow thee: therefore also that holy thing which shall be born of thee shall be called the Son of God. And behold, thy cousin Elizabeth, she hath also conceived a son in her old age: and this is the sixth month with her, who was called barren. For with God nothing shall be impossible. And Mary said, Behold the handmaid of the Lord; be it unto me according to thy word. And the angel departed from her.

(The Gospel According to St. Luke, *1:26-38*)

A large hall for celebrations takes up the upper level of the building, spiral stairs in the towers on the façade and a star-shaped opening in the middle of the room leads to the lower level.

The choir with the new altar that was added after some modifications to the original plans, so that it meets the new liturgical canons suggested by the Ecumenical Council Vatican II.

THE UPPER BASILICA

It is obvious that the builder wanted to distinguish the upper part of the basilica from the simplicity of the crypt. Large windows fill the big room with light, and the visitors' eyes are practically overwhelmed by artworks. The "unfinished" bare cement does not actually diminish the magnificence of this church. The big central "oculus" gives the building a sense of unity, by creating a physical link between the oldest relics in the crypt and airy height of the dome, covered with prefabricated panelling. Major international celebrations are held here, as is daily worship for the local, Roman catholic population. The church fills up completely on some of the most solemn occasions such as the Good Friday procession which is an important religious event for the local Arab Christian community.

The inlays on the central marble pavement, by the Italian artist Adriano Alessandrini of Rome, depict Mary's prerogatives as recognized by the Ecumenical Councils starting with the Council of Ephesus (431 A.D.) and papal decrees.

Along the walls, going clockwise, after the panel dedicated to Marian sanctuaries entrusted to the Sons of St. Francis, are paintings from Cameroon, Hungary, Taiwan, Venezuela, Brazil, Poland, the United States of America, Portugal, Spain, France, Canada, Japan, Mexico, Australia, Lebanon, England and Italy.

Marian themes are interpreted through the most varied artistic techniques and with different cultural influences: artists from many countries created the pictures that decorate the walls.

The back walls of the choir are decorated with a majestic mosaic by the painter Salvatore Fiume of Canzo, Italy. In the center, Christ spreads his arms towards all humanity that is going to him. At his side, stands Peter who has received the keys to the kingdom of heaven. In the lower right portion of the mosaic are the popes who governed the Church from 1917 to 1968: Benedict XV, Pius XI, Pius XII, John XXIII and Paul VI.

The chapel on the left is dedicated to St. Francis (the graffito with the scene of the saint receiving the stigmata was done by the Italian painter, Glauco Baruzzi of Milan) and the Franciscan order to which the Holy See assigned custodianship of the holy places in 1342, thus confirming what the sovereigns of Naples, Charles of Anjou and his wife, Sancia of Majorca had managed to obtain from the Sultan through extensive diplomatic negotiations and enormous outlays of money.

The chapel on the right, where the Holy Sacrament is kept, is dedicated to all the saints, and in particular those of Palestine. The paintings, by the Spanish artist Rafael Ubeda of Pontevedra develop the theme of universal reconciliation as the final phase in the struggle between good and evil that embraces all humanity in its difficult journey on this earth. An expression of this effort at reconciliation is the scene of the historic embrace between Pope Paul VI and Athenagoras I, patriarch of Constantinople during the pope's pilgramage to the Holy Land in 1964.

Preceding page, bottom: the mosaic in the choir focuses on the church, which according to the words of the "Creed" at the top is, "One, Holy, Catholic and Apostolic".

The two chapels at the sides of the choir: one dedicated to the preservation of holy relics, especially of Franciscan saints, and the other contains the Holy Sacrament.

Light is a highly symbolic element. The artist's skill is evident in his ability to mediate between the material and the spiritual worlds, by carefully distributing light and color inside this sacred building.

The stained glass windows of the upper basilica were made by the French artist Max Ingrand of Paris. The Annunciation is depicted on the southern façade and is indirectly portrayed on the western side as well, above the main façade, inside a composition of pointed arches that recall the masterpieces of Medieval Gothic cathedrals. For the 33 windows of the outside walls, the artist took his inspiration from the Song of Songs. Although the main theme of this poetic book is human love, according to Jewish tradition it can be read in allegorical terms as the religious message of God's love for Israel, His chosen people. Christian tradition sees the beloved bride as the Church, the faithful soul in general and Mary in particular. The windows of the dome, made of concrete framed glass blocks by the Swiss artist Yoki Aebischer of Fribourg portray the apostles, Mary's parents Joachim and Anne, St. Ephrem the Syrian and St. Bernard of Clairvaux.

Perhaps the dome is the most original and characteristic part of the entire building. Seen from the inside it recalls an enormous flower, while from the outside it resembles a royal crown.

The central cupola of the church rises above the reinforced concrete bearing walls that were designed to withstand both temperature changes and the not uncommon seismic events that occur in the area.

The inside of the dome is made of prefabricated panels decorated with a continuous zig-zag motif that can also be interpreted as an infinite repetition of the "M" for Mary or Messiah, in this case Jesus. The panels arranged in a ray simulate an enormous lilly with white petals and with a corolla that equals the maximum inside diameter of the dome (21 meters). The cupola appears to by symbolically filled with light that comes not only from the central opening of the lantern, but mainly from the sixteen triangular windows that open where the petals taper at the support point of the octagonal drum. This circle of intense light creates a special effect of weightlessness, as if the dome were suspended above the building rather than being supported by it. The comparison with the flower brings to mind a spontaneous reference to the etymological meaning of the name Nazareth. Several sources say that it comes from the Hebrew root "nezer", for flower or sprout. The word appears in Isaiah's prophecy (11:1-2) that heralds the rise of "a rod out of the stem of Jesse", that is the Messiah from the house of David. St. Jerome used similar words around 400 A.D. when he wrote to the Roman noblewoman, Marcella," We shall go to Nazareth and we shall see, in accordance with the meaning of its name, the flower of the Galilee."

The outside of the dome is covered with stone up to the open gallery, 27 meters above the ground. The gallery and the lantern are made of stone, while the pyramid is copper clad.

There is an intermediate airspace between the double coverings. And this space provides access to all the levels of the dome (it is not open to the public) up to the skylight, 55 meters above the lower basilica's entrance portico.

The new baptistry rises above the covered courtyard. It's a small, separate chapel, outside of the main building, as once required by ancient church tradition.

Two doors lead from the upper basilica to the covered courtyard. The subjects on the bronze doors made by the sculptor Niel Steenberger of Weert, The Netherlands are *Ecclesia ex Circumsione*, or the Jewish Origins of the Church (with Jesse's tree, the Annunciation, the Adoration of the Shepherds and the Call of Peter) and *Ecclesia ex Gentibu*s, or the Church of those who converted from paganism (with the cycle of the prophet Jonah, the Adoration of the Magi, Pentecost and the Conversion of Saul). Glazed ceramic inserts (by the sculptor Angelo Biancini of Faenza, Italy) with scenes of the Nativity and the Adoration of the Magi decorate the tympanums of the doors. The chapel-baptistry is a true jewel of Christian art. The complex was created by a married couple (Bernd Hartmann-Lintel and Irma Rochelle of Wiedenbrück, Germany) who work in bronze and mosaic. It depicts the Baptism of Jesus in the Jordan River, while the Holy Spirit descends on the Messiah in the form of a dove.

Arrangements can be made to visit the archeological area situated below the covered courtyard of the basilica. What remains of the ancient village of Nazareth is basically a network of grottoes and bits of walls from various historical periods. Going backwards in time we first see the remains of the XVII century Franciscan monastery, then the palace of the crusader archbishop of Nazareth and humble homes with some parts datable from at least the IX-VIII cent. B.C. The homes that were carved into the soft local rock are the best preserved: we can see cisterns for storing rainwater, silos on several levels for storing foodstuffs, a winepress, cellars for full jugs, stables with mangers for the livestock, a bread-oven...The part farthest to the east is traditionally known as the "Virgin's kitchen" because of its proximity to the sacred grotto.

Remains of the ancient village of Nazareth, and mainly its grottoes, with an oven for baking bread.

Photo on the right: detail of a headless bust of St. Peter.

The museum contains the main items found during the excavations that preceded construction of the modern basilica.

Preceding page: fragments of sculptures that decorated the crusader basilica destroyed in 1263.

Octagonal decorated capitals (XII cent.) with scenes from the lives of the apostles Peter, James, Matthew and Thomas (from top to bottom, left to right). The scene depicted on the rectangular capital (bottom photo) is open to several interpretations.

MUSEUM

The local Museum, established by Father Prosper Viaud around 1910 contains some objects found in tombs around the city, and which illustrate Nazareth's early history. The excavations from 1955-60 provided invaluable epigraphic evidence that is displayed in the showcases on the sides: Greek, Latin and Armenian graffito inscriptions made by IV-V century pilgrims. The artistic highlight of the collection is the magnificent group of carved capitals (XII cent) that were found by accident in a grotto on the grounds of the Franciscan monastery in 1909.

Going along the Franciscan monastery, we come to the Church of Joseph, also known as the Church of the Nutrition or of the Holy Family. Archeological finds from various basilicas and sacred buildings are placed throughout the garden along the pilgrims' path.

CHURCH OF JOSEPH

The impressive structure that houses the Franciscan monastery was designed by Brother Johann Schoppen (1930). The Franciscan order, which has been in Nazareth on an official basis since 1620, is entrusted with the custodianship of the basilica and Roman Catholic parish which currently has about 5,000 members. The order's pastoral duties include many social and charitable activities such as the home for senior citizens, which has its headquarters in the Chapel of Our Lady of the Fright. The famous Terra Sancta College which takes up the entire northern portion of the monastery building has its roots in the XVII century, as we can see from contemporary sources :"In Jerusalem, Bethlehem and Nazareth, schooling shall be provided for the parish boys up to the age of 9, they shall be given a midday meal, and in the evening shall return to their homes." Today the school is open to all, and it educates boys and girls from kindergarten to the threshold of the university.

Preceding page, top: interior of the Church of Joseph; bottom: oil painting of the Holy Family by the French artist, François Lafond of Toulouse (1896).

Crypt in the Church of Joseph, with the mosaic inlaid basin believed to be an old baptismal font.

The church of Joseph, in an imitation romantic style was designed by Brother Wendelin Hinterkeuser (1911) and built over an earlier crusader church (XII cent) parts of which can still be seen in the façade. The holy memory is suggested by the tradition of "St. Joseph's workshop", that the Franciscans found at the site in the XVII century, or the word of a second church in Nazareth dedicated to "nourishing Jesus", that we can read in the account of Arculf's pilgrimage (VIII cent).

Various views of the old city, with the Basilica of the Annunciation in the foreground (upper left), the convent of the Dames de Nazareth (bottom left), the Greek Catholic church (top) and the city's old mosque (below).

THE OLD CITY

Members of many different faiths and religions live together in Nazareth in a fine example of tolerance. Alongside of the new Basilica of the Annunciation that belongs to the Roman Catholics, we see the Greek Catholic church of the Annunciation, right in the middle of the town, and slightly further along stands the Maronite Catholic church of St. Anthony Abbot. Next to it stands the Anglican church and the old mosque, known as *al-Abyad*, "the white one". Near the spring, at the end of the city's main street rises the Greek Orthodox Church of the Annunciation, farther down is the American Baptist church. The Egyptian Coptic church is on a side street, next to the new *as-Salam* mosque "of Peace". The call of the *muezzins* and the sound of the bells often blend, and follow each other, especially at dusk when the carillon at the top of the basilica gently plays out the melody of the *Ave* of Nazareth.

This page and following pages: the typical narrow streets of the town center, closed to traffic, where the small market thrives with all the charm and bustle of an Oriental bazaar.

THE MARKET

The life of the *souk* (market) is always very lively, involving not only the city's residents, but on certain days people from nearby villages, Arabs and Jews alike. Naturally, foreign tourists in search of souvenirs find everything that can arouse their curiosity, especially near the holy places: illustrated books (like this one), wooden and metal wares, pottery, decorated T-shirts and *keffiahs* the typical Arab headcovering. The merchants, in accordance with Eastern customs, display all their wares in an orderly disarray to attract all kinds of customers with the lure of a bargain; the prices are usually good and can be "negotiated" with the merchant. The once flourishing artisans are finding themselves obliged to move to other parts of town that are easier to reach by car or public transportation, and this, in turn helps economic growth.

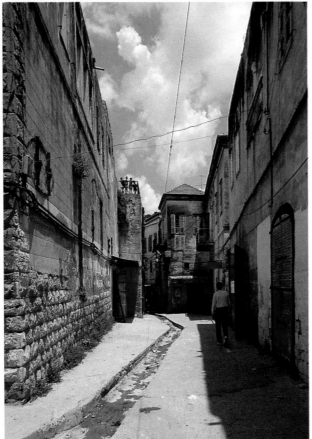

Just a short distance from the Basilica of the Annunciation stands the protestant church (Anglican) that recently underwent extensive restorations.

Baptismal font carved in local stone.

PROTESTANT CHURCH

The Episcopalian Evangelical Christ Church of Nazareth founded in 1871 is an outstanding monument in old Nazareth. From the architectural standpoint the building is based on northern European and mainly English Gothic models, in accordance with the origins of the church itself. Its membership and clergy, however, include people from the local Arab population (approximately 800). Anglican pilgrims, like others who came to the holy places found hospitality in the Franciscan monastery as we can see from the signatures on some stones in the local museum and the pilgrims registry (*Navis Peregrinorum*).

The list of distinguished visitors includes Robert Maundreil pastor of the Anglican church in Aleppo, Syria, who wrote a book describing the journey he made in 1697.

The Anglican community in Nazareth runs a school and a home for the elderly (St. Margaret's Home). A recent addition to Nazareth's many religious communities is the Baptists and the Church of the Nazarene.

CASA NOVA

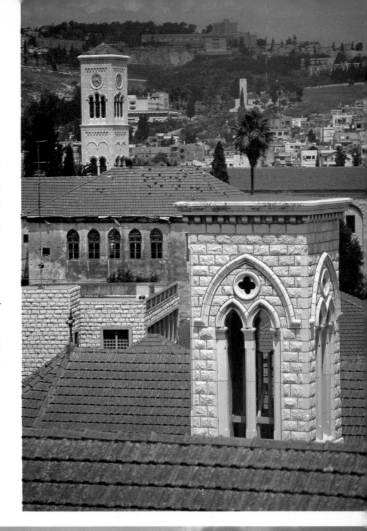

In past centuries the city of Nazareth did not have any real guest facilities aside from the Eastern caravanserai; Christian pilgrims usually found lodgings in a part of the Franciscan monastery specifically set aside for them. Sometime around 1830 a new building was erected next to the monastery (hence the name "Casa Nova" or new house) which was replaced by the existing one in 1897. Today visitors can find comfortable accommodations in one of the many hotels of all categories that are run by the local population, for whom tourists are an important source of income.

Next to the Casa Nova, when the convent of the Dames de Nazareth was being built in 1855, remains of a Medieval structure and a first century Jewish tomb, carved into the rock with a revolving stone over the entrance were found. This is one of the finest known examples of this type of gravesite. The Dames de Nazareth operate a school for the blind and deaf. Many other social services flourish in Nazareth: a school for the disabled was established by the Opera Pia Don Guanella in 1974.

Opposite page and above: four views of the convent of the Dames de Nazareth.

Below "Casa Nova", the oldest pilgrims' hospice in Nazareth.

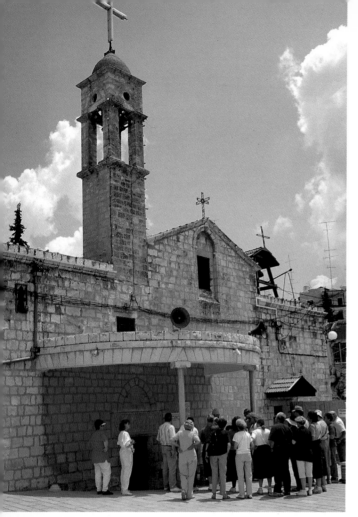

CHURCH OF GABRIEL

At the edges of the hill, over which the old village once rose, to the northeast there is still an abundant spring known as "Mary's spring" (*'ain sitti Mariam*). We can suppose that the Virgin, like every other woman of Nazareth, often came to this spring for household water. The water springs from the rock about 30 meters from the church; a duct carries it into the church and then to the monumental fountain on the road to Tiberias.

In addition to being a sanctuary, Gabriel's Church is the parish church of the Greek Orthodox community, which is the largest of the Arab-Christian congregations in Nazareth with over 14,000 members. It is run by a Greek bishop who answers to the Patriarch of Jerusalem and it has a lively Orthodox Social Center that organizes all sorts of community activities.

Entrance to the Greek Orthodox church of the Annunciation, which the pilgrims call St. Gabriel, and a stone with a commemorative inscription in Arabic.

Interior of Gabriel's church; view of the apse with the altar for celebrating mass and the beautiful ciborium.

The existing church dates from 1750 when the Orthodox Greeks obtained a firman from the Turkish sultan of Constantinople granting them permission to rebuild the old, ruined church. Previously, all Christian worship was held in the undergound tunnel where the mouth of the spring is located. With its three, nearly windowless naves and square bell tower that is topped by a luminous cross, it represents the typical image of the old Eastern rite churches scattered throughout the Galilee. In the XII century the Russian pilgrim, Daniel, wrote about a round church: "As we left the city, heading east, we came to a remarkable, deep well with very cold water; one can go down into it by steps. A round church, dedicated to St. Gabriel covers the well."

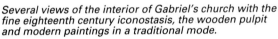

Several views of the interior of Gabriel's church with the fine eighteenth century iconostasis, the wooden pulpit and modern paintings in a traditional mode.

The north wall contains the opening that leads to the mouth of the spring.

In 1767 the carved and gilded wooden iconostasis was put into the church. It was a gift of a Greek merchant on pilgrimage to Nazareth, and according to the inscription in Arabic and Greek, it was made by Andrew di Maistu. Fine icons from the school of Jerusalem depict the Savior Enthroned, the Virgin and Child, St. John the Baptist with angel wings; St. George on horseback, and other images of the saints most venerated by Christians in Palestine. Recently, all the walls were redecorated by two Romanian artists, Michel and Gabriel Marosan. The painted scenes, mainly from the Old and New Testaments, are lively and colorful, so that they blend well with the rest of the building.

Tempera painting of the Annunciation at the well: in the arch above the entrance to the tunnel.

Below and right: the tunnel with stone-faced ceiling; the walls are decorated with eighteenth century majolica and inlaid marble panels in elegant trefoil arches; at the end, in the absidiole, is the mouth of the spring.

MARY'S WELL

This place preserves the memory of the Annunciation, which according to ancient eastern tradition, as substantiated by the Protevangelium of James (an apocryphal text dating from the II century A.D.): "[Mary]came with a pitcher to fetch water. And she heard a voice: Hail, thou that art highly favored, the Lord is with thee: blessed art thou among women". The angel's greeting (*Luke* 1:28) is embellished by the enthusiastic words of Elizabeth (*Luke* 1:42) as in the traditional Hail Mary prayer.

Exterior view and the interior of the church of Jesus the Adolescent built atop the hill overlooking the city of Nazareth (top right).

The vocational school run by the Salesians of Don Bosco: main façade.

Nazareth seen from the top of the hill.

THE SALESIAN CHURCH

The Salesian fathers who had been running an orphanage in Nazareth since 1896 (Home of Jesus the Adolescent) were able to settle permanently on the hill overlooking the city in 1902. Later they built the neo-Gothic church, designed by the French architect Lucien Gauther. The church is dedicated to Jesus the Adolescent who, in this city "increased in wisdom and stature, and in favor with God and man" according to the Gospel (*Luke* 2:52). In the beginning the home was characterized by its predominantly French orientation, but since 1948 the school is open to all. It is mainly technical and vocational and is equipped with woodworking and metal shops, and now recently, has added courses in electronics and computer skills. Its aim, in accordance with the words of Don Bosco is to educate young people so they take their place in society with dignity and become "honest citizens and good Christians.

The church commemorating the miracle of the transformation of water into wine. View of the main façade, the interior and the crypt of the Franciscan church.

CANA

The name of Cana appears in the Gospel according to John on three separate occasions (*John* 2:1-11; 4:46; 21:2) and it is always followed by "of Galilee", to distinguish it from the other Cana on the border of Phoenicia (Lebanon). At Cana Jesus transformed water into wine during the wedding feast to which he had been invited with his disciples and his mother, Mary. This was the first of his miracles; at Cana a royal official obtained a cure for his son who was lying ill at Capernaum; and finally Nathaniel, who according to tradition is the apostle Bartholomew, came from Cana.

Until the XVII century there were doubts as to whether the biblical Cana was at Khirbet Qana or Kefr Kenna, two towns about 8 kilometers apart. Pilgrims usually stopped at one of these places, according to the times. Of the two, Kefr Kenna still stands today, where the nearby Greek-Orthodox (1886) and Franciscan (1879) church commemorate the miracle of Cana of Galilee by displaying sym-

bolic stone hydria. The Franciscan church was built with some ancient architectural pieces, and there is a mosaic with an Aramaic inscription: "Remember Joseph, son of Tanhum, son of Butah with his sons because they made this *tabula*; may they be blessed. Amen". Aside from the difficulty in interpreting the key word in the text which we have given here as "tabula", the inscription is evidence of an ancient Jewish community and also probably a house of worship. Recent excavations (1969) in the north courtyard and adjacent rooms have brought to light other mosaics and ancient walls from a synagogue with a south-facing façade.

At the entrance to the village is the spring that is believed to be the source of the water that Jesus changed into wine. St. Bartholomew is commemorated in a chapel at the end of the city, near the school run by the Franciscan Missionary Sisters of the Immaculate Heart of Mary.

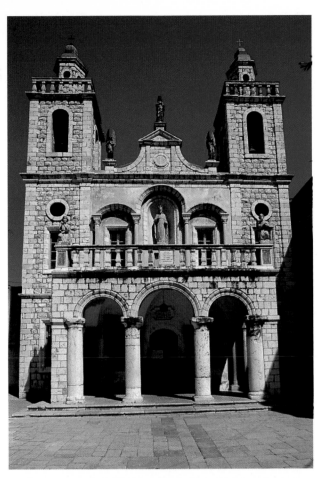

Mount Tabor rises above the plain of Esdraelon.

The facade of the Church of the Transfiguration and its fortified entrance.

Following pages: the interior of the church, the mosaic in the absidal vault depicting the Transfiguration and the crypt.

MOUNT TABOR

The Gospel does not tell us the name of the mountain where the Transfiguration took place before the eyes of Jesus' favorite disciples, Peter, John and James when, as he prayed "the fashion of his countenance was altered and his raiment was white and glistening." and Moses and Elias appeared before him and spoke "of his decease which he should accomplish at Jerusalem" (Luke 9:28-36). Starting from the III century, Christian tradition has held that the place was Mount Tabor (*Har Tavor* in Hebrew, *Jebel et-Tur* in Arabic), which because of its isolated position and aura of biblical holiness was well suited to host the three churches and monasteries built to celebrate this Gospel event in the Byzantine period (V-VII cent.).

A long and narrow road winds along the rocky, oak-covered slopes. The flattened peak, is still surrounded by the remains of the walls of the Saracen fortress (XIII cent.). At the eastern end rises the basilica (1924) designed by the architect Antonio

Barluzzi who was inspired by the ancient churches of northern Syria. The modern church follows the outlines of the crusader and Byzantine buildings that came before. Ruins of the earlier structures can still be seen in the church's crypt, in the chapel next to the entrance portico on the southern side, and in the sacristy. The northern and southern chapels are dedicated to Moses, the lawgiver and Elias, the prophet, respectively.

The ruins surrounding the church consist primarily of bits of the Benedictine monastery from the crusader period (XII cent.). Next to the Franciscan property of the custody of the Holy Land is the Greek-Orthodox land, with its church built in 1845 dedicated to St. Elias.The view from the top of Mount Tabor is unique. One can see from the snowy peaks of Mt. Hermon to the spurs of Mt. Carmel, to the sea and then to the Plain of Esdraelon revisiting the biblical towns of Megiddo, Iezreel and Naim where Jesus performed one of his miracles.

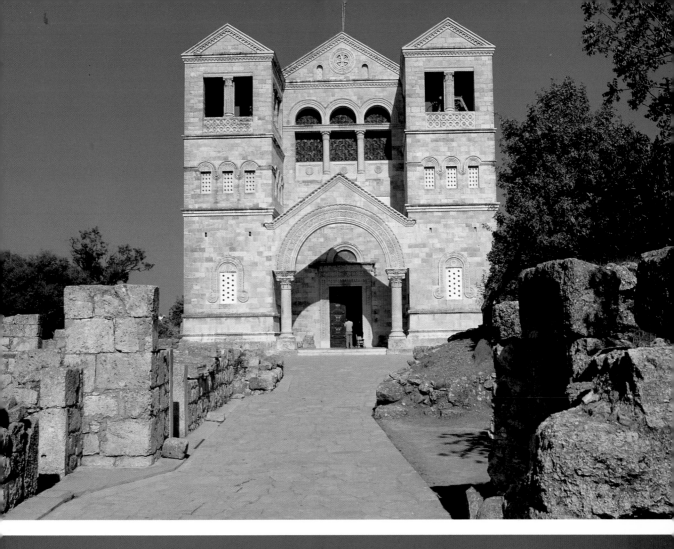

Visitors gaze into the deep trenches of the Megiddo tell. Archeologists have brought to light traces of ancient civilizations dating back 6,000 years.

Top right: the round Canaanite altar made of rough stone is reached by a short flight of steps.

MEGIDDO

In Palestine, the sites of ancient buried cities can often be recognized by a typical flat-topped artificial hill. These "tells" are usually formed by layers of ruins from different eras that gradually accumulate.

The biblical city of Megiddo was recognized in the artificial hill known as *Tel Mutesellim* that rises near the edges of the fertile Plain of Esdraelon. Various teams of archeologists, German (1903-1905), American (1925-1935) and Israeli (1960-1970) have dug and brought to light remains from at least 20 "layers" or "levels of occupation". The city's importance can be seen from the size of the tell, and is

easily explained by its geographic position. It was located so that it could control the main trading route from the ancient east, known as the Via Maris, the road to the sea. Therefore, it is easy to understand why Megiddo was the scene of the main battles for the possession of Palestine from ancient times up to the present. The book of the *Apocalypse* (16:16) mentions Armageddon, which would be Megiddo, in relation to the final battle of the Antichrist.

In the Old Testament Megiddo is a Canaanite city at the time of the conquest (*Joshua*, 12:21); King Solomon fortified it (*I Kings,* 4:21); the kings of

Judah, Ahaziah and Josiah died there in battle (*II Kings*, 9:27; 23:29). The military importance of the site is also evident from its Roman name of *Legio* it was the headquarters of VI Legion "Ferrata" after the Jewish revolt of 66-70 A.D.

The first human settlement dates from the second half of the IV millenium B.C. with ruins of rectangular or absidial houses made of raw bricks that were found in Layer XX. Afterwards, the city seems to be better organized with a defensive wall over 8 meters thick, built of sun-baked bricks on a stone foundation and a *bamah* (high place).

The public granary from the Assyrian period, with a double staircase.

Remains of walls, channels and stone basins from the ancient dwellings of Megiddo.

This was an outdoor circular platform, 8 meters in diameter, 1.5 meters high, made of rough stones, with steps along the side and used for worship and sacrifices. Between 1400 and 1100 B.C., the city was violenty destroyed and among the ruins of its palaces archeologists have found remarkable artistic treasures: inlaid ivories and jewels that represent the best of Canaanite art from the period. From the era in which the Israelites ruled over the city, that is from the days of King Solomon (layers VI to IV; 950-733 B.C.) there are remains of the fortifications with casemate walls, and mainly two large stables capable of housing up to 492 horses. Each consists of a long room with two rows of columns, to which the horses were tied, down the center. The pillars were evenly spaced and designed to support the roof. The most recent studies also attribute the excavation of an elaborate underground structure to this period. It consists of a well, 25 meters deep and a 70 meter long tunnel which assured access to the fresh-water spring.

The granary (12 meters wide and 7 meters deep) with two spiral staircases dates from after the Assyrian conquest (733 B.C.).

TABLE OF CONTENTS